Living with PTSD

Journey of a Veteran

Accompaniment to the exhibition

by

Villayat 'SnowMoon Wolf' Sunkmanitu

Paperback ISBN: 978-0-9564885-4-1
Also available on Amazon Kindle

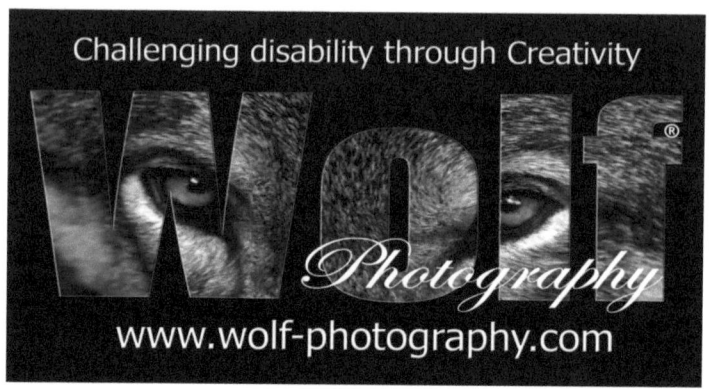

Wolf Photography is a 'Not-for-Profit' company. Funds raised from this project are used to carry out creative work and raise more awareness of how PTSD affects people. The project also raises awareness of how creativity can help people cope with a disability and educates people about their Intellectual Property rights.

SnowMoon Wolf is the publishing wing of the project.

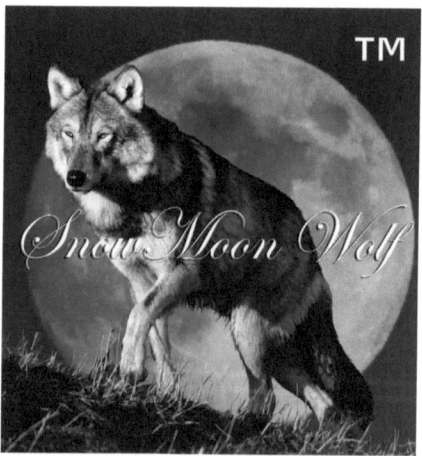

Contents

Living with Post Traumatic Stress Disorder (PTSD)
The idea for an exhibition

It started just over six years ago. People that know of my photography were asking when I would be exhibiting again. Something inside kept saying 'not yet' and I waited. The concept was clear though: to raise awareness of what it's like to live with PTSD and to promote creativity as a coping mechanism.

In the meantime I was enduring a traumatic move from Cornwall to Nottingham. Traumatic because I had to move away from my son and daughter.

Traumatic because one health authority within the NHS didn't trust another and so disregarded the reports compiled just before the move – reports that were to facilitate a transfer of care from one part of the UK to another. Their policy was to make their own assessment and I didn't feel like being re-assessed.

Every time someone wants to forcibly pry into my past it opens up the scars and brings the trauma more to the fore. It hurts and it completely disrupts all of my coping mechanisms … thus pressing my triggers and putting me on the edge.

While I understand that the system has a duty to ensure that War Disablement Pensions and other benefits are being paid to those eligible … I don't understand the need to conduct inhumane interviews when there is a large amount of consistent documentary evidence available.

If you have disabled Veterans under your care … please be respectful, be aware of their needs and allow them to cope with the difficulties that they face without stripping away any dignity that they're left with, after having already gone through your assessments once.

Acknowledgment

This exhibition wouldn't be possible without the grants awarded by the Arts Council England and the National Lottery.

I'd also like to thank the people that have supported me in my work over the years, both online and in person, past and present.

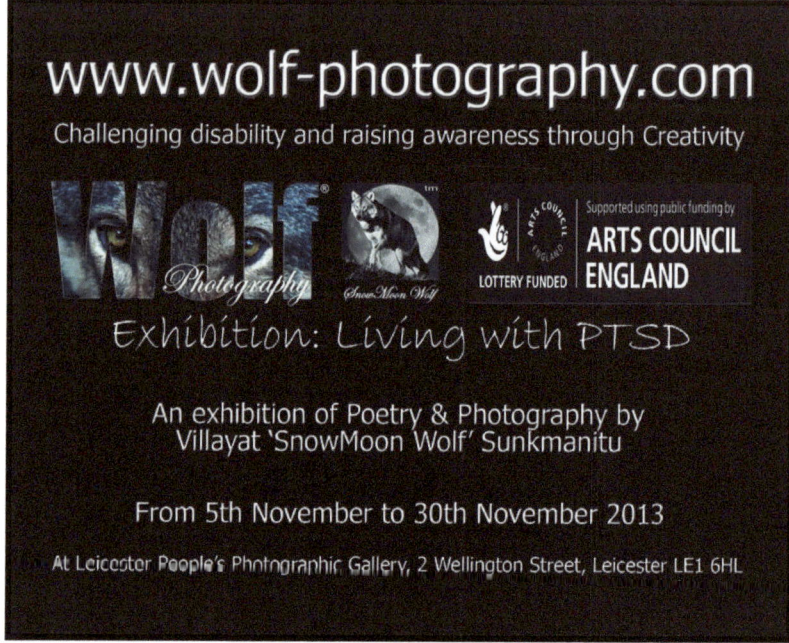

Primarily, this book was put together for the people that can't attend the exhibition whether it be because of disability or their geographical location. I love looking at the 'Flag Counter' on my web page and seeing which countries people visit from. The world has become a smaller place.

I hope that some of you will feel that the book warrants a space in your home as a keepsake of the exhibition but more importantly, I hope that if you live with PTSD, you won't feel quite so alone ... and maybe you'll venture forth on your own creative journey via whichever form of art floats your boat.

8

Background

I served with the Royal Air Force Police between 1981 – 1985. The first two year posting after training was great – RAF St Mawgan in Cornwall – such a beautiful place!

In those years St Mawgan was operational and had a lot going on. We still had Shackletons flying – great big planes with four propeller engines that were capable of staying out on missions for a twenty four hour period.

We also had the Nimrods there as well as Wessex and Sea King helicopters in the Search and Rescue role. I don't know how many lives they saved over the years between them … but it was a privilege to be part of the team that protected them when they were on the ground. They were the heroes.

We still had Canberras as well and regular visitors from other units (Eg Tornados, Hawks, Chinooks, Harriers, Bucaneers, Herky birds) and various UN countries that afforded 'propellor heads' like me (people that love aircraft - particularly fast movers) a chance to watch them. I used to love photographing them, particularly on exercises or airshows.

We had a few 'brown trouser' moments when aircraft with live munitions would come in with various problems such as part of the undercarriage being jammed inoperable. Serious incidents were avoided through the skill and courage of the pilots involved in those episodes.

Guess what floated my boat more than aircraft photography? The lovely scenery in the area and … WILDLIFE!

Whether it's fauna or flora, mammals or insects … each had its challenges and focussing on the art took away any stresses or strains and allowed me to immerse myself into a world where there was nothing but awe and wonder at the colours and forms provided by the natural world.

I was posted to County down in Northern Ireland in 1983. I stopped taking photographs within three months of getting there. Something had changed within me but I wasn't quite sure what it was.

I had acclimatised to the seriousness of serving in Northern Ireland, I had been involved in a few incidents ... and I had been subjected to racism by a Senior Non-Commissioned Officer and his sidekick.

I understood the situation that we were involved in as the 'Security Forces' ... as well as the way that we were hampered from carrying out our duties by politicians ... on both sides of the water ... and, I suspect, by high ranking officials that were playing politics instead of being responsible leaders.

There are things that I cannot relate to you because of the Official Secrets Act ... and there are things that I'm trying to forget ... but they keep clawing their way back into the shadowy corridors of my mind ... making their presence felt while they drag me back – sometimes kicking and shouting to some of those scenarios that play like a video tape that's stuck ... leaving me fighting under the covers as I relive the moments and try to fight my way out of the situation(s) ... fighting to break loose of the shadowy world of the nightmare to come back to being fully awake.

As the tour in Northern Ireland progressed I became disillusioned with the military – it had become clear in my mind that while local briefings carried a certain set of instructions and goals with regards to the arrest of terrorists ... deals were being made in the halls of power that failed to underline and support the objective. As a result, I submitted my papers to leave the RAF when I finished my two year tour of Northern Ireland.

I knew something was wrong with me ... but I didn't know what it was called or the circumstances that led to its existence ... that is, with hindsight, I knew that the incidents I was involved in had something to do with it ... but I was completely unaware of the mechanics of the condition.

10

After leaving the RAF Police, I served in the Metropolitan Police. My career was cut very short after being involved in an incident that involved a small explosion. You can read about the specifics in 'The Way of the Wolf' – the poem is called 'Sacrifice of Youth'. I have no doubt that racism played its part in the way in which I was treated by both the Metropolitan Police and the Crown Prosecution Service at the time.

My next career path took me into the area of civil human rights via the Citizens' Advice Bureau (CAB). I remember interviewing clients with complex problems and recognising myself within the symptoms being recorded … it was old pattern to lock my emotions away though and focus on helping others. It's easier to help others and I wasn't ready to open my particular can of worms.

In 1995 I was lucky to have survived a serious road accident … but the damage that my body had sustained took away my one coping mechanism … Shotokan Karate. I hadn't touched a camera or walked the Earth with one in years. The nightmares and flashbacks intensified and I was being driven to the edge by the circumstances I found myself in, so I contacted my doctor and asked for help.

I was very fortunate that my doctor was switched on. He connected the dots, questioned me about my past – much to my bemusement – and made a referral to the local mental health team.

After the diagnoses I was both relieved and further angered. I was angry at the MoD and the RAF for not screening me and telling me that I had contracted PTSD as a result of my duties in the Armed Forces. I felt betrayed.

I had done everything that they had asked of me to prepare for the role they wanted me to play … and I had put my life on the line on a few occasions.

I took very few photographs during this period of illumination. I was having a hard time coping with the truth of the situation.

After 10 years in the CAB Service I went to work in the NHS as an IT engineer. I needed a complete break from fighting cases.

During this time I started to play around with digital cameras and I started to build up a collection of images that I'd share for free on 'Webshots' ... until two work colleagues asked my why I wasn't selling my photography. I actually thought they were making fun of me and that my photography wasn't anything to make a song and dance about. They persevered with my attitude though and eventually talked me round. I set up my first website – www.wolf1964.co.uk on 24th December 2002. My colleagues became my first customers and I had a second occupation that brought me much peace and pleasure.

A little while later, Wolf Photography came into existence, following my education about the nature of the Wolf from some Native American (First Nations) teachers. I was also taught how to cope with PTSD using 'Earth Medicine'.

I was eventually retired on ill health from the NHS in 2006 and slowly, as I've become more aware of the plight of Veterans that have served from England , Northern Ireland, Scotland and Wales ... I knew that I wanted to try to help raise some awareness of how we're treated by the system. I also wanted to continue travelling the world and photograph wild animals and wilderness areas.

Seeking help is hard work

I remember when the scars were opened … it was during a ceremony with a group called 'Ehama'. They're a group of teachers from different tribes in North America that came together to try to support, enable and teach people to use the Medicine of the Earth in order to cope with various difficulties that affect the mind, body and spirit.

They reached me in ways that the NHS couldn't.

The NHS model was to provide me with Cognitive Behavioural Therapy (CBT) and some Eye Movement Desensitization and Reprocessing (EMDR) sessions.

We're all wired differently. I found the CBT useful but the EMDR made me want to do physical harm to the practitioner.

The only other thing the NHS do is prescribe pills. That's something that I stay away from where possible. I'd seen so many of the lads at Combat Stress complain of feeling like zombies because of the medication they were on. That's not a route that I wanted to go down.

I do however use herbal medicines: St John's Wort and Valerian.

In order to get the help that we need, we have to bare our souls to the system and it's not a pleasant experience; particularly when you consider that we played the role of 'helper', operated in some tough conditions and were relied upon to do our utmost to help protect others.

Perhaps it's just pride that gets in the way … but pride and our conditioning from day one at 'square bashing' stopped us behaving like 'civvies'. We turned into people that would go until we literally dropped – in the main. Giving up was no longer an option … because we had to look after our brothers and we had to get each other out of tricky situations. We were hard working, motivated, professional people. So when we go to an NHS environment and are subjected to less than professional behaviour from therapists and their support staff ... it colours our perception of how much use they can be to us. Add to this one other piece of data: the NHS don't know how to cope with fighters ... most of the people that they help have given up and are at their lowest and so pop the pills they're given. The average Veteran will keep fighting ... they live amongst emotional peaks and troughs - the wiser of them trying to find a balanced middle ground between the two so as to avoid having to constantly go between what can sometimes be an alarming change in mood.

It takes a lot for a Veteran to ask for help ... yet very few agencies appropriately prioritise their needs. If you're a Veteran with a disability that requires medical treatment for the condition that you were awarded a War Disablement Pension, you're entitled to be prioritised on the waiting list for treatment. Most NHS administrators are ignorant of this. We obviously can't be prioritised over an urgent case ... but most aren't given any priority treatment at all; you're also entitled to free medication for your specific condition.

It can be soul destroying to be on a waiting list for a mental health practitioner – you could be waiting a long time if they're unaware of the above information relating to Veterans. It's not unheard of for a Veteran to be waiting months if not years for access to appropriate help. It's a sliding scale of severity of disability and budgetary constraints.

If you need help, make sure someone from somewhere is supporting you emotionally that is independent of the care provider.

First visit to Combat Stress

It's not something that I'll probably ever forget. I'd driven over from my home in Cornwall. The drive was uneventful and I was focussed on the task of driving rather than what going to Combat Stress meant.

I arrived at the gates and I felt really unsure about going in. Something deep inside rebelled against this course of action.

It took the staff about fifteen minutes to talk me in over the intercom – it felt a lot longer than that.

I had a brilliant 'key worker' assigned to me as well as a specialist that both allowed me the space to escape if I felt overwhelmed by being there.

I was like a trapped animal and couldn't hack being in the building. I kept going outside to stop myself from shaking and rebelling ... and the only place I felt safe was inside a large tree that had a natural hollow in its trunk. I'd curl up in there and just let the energy of the tree soothe me, protect me ... calm me. The therapists could talk to me there and start the work of unlocking all the memories ... some that were buried so deep that I couldn't believe they were my experiences.

I learned to cope though ... with their help ... and so will you.

Don't give up. You're not alone any more. There are others that know how you feel ... maybe not exactly ... but close enough to allow you to feel that bond again.

You also have to be prepared for the feeling of separation again ... because at the end of your brief stay, you'll go back to your life and you'll go back to coping ... and it can feel as raw as the time that you left the mob all those years ago ... and you'll miss your mates all over again.

Loved ones and Veterans

For the reasons mentioned in the last sections, most Veterans won't discuss their experiences with loved ones. It can be problematic if they're involved in loving relationships because once where there was openness, there can now be a wall that's higher than Everest ... and equally hard to climb.

If you're involved with or related to a Veteran that you care about, don't ever push them to tell you anything as it could trigger a negative reaction. Just let them know that they're still loved and that you're there for them should they wish to talk.

You may find that they will stay at home more and more, venturing out only for necessary tasks ... preferring their safe zone. Don't pressure them ... if they feel like staying in – let them. They'll venture out when they're ready.

Be especially careful in times of high general stress on the family unit (eg unemployment, moving house, dealing with debt, other health problems, relationship problems etc).

Veterans need to remember that it's hard for your loved ones if you shut them out; assuming they want to be a part of the Veterans' lives. Real love is unconditional ... and if our behaviour causes pain to our loved ones, the wounds can be deep. The people around Veterans will know that person has changed and that it has something to do with military service and incidents experienced in the various operations they may have served in ... but they won't understand the real issues unless they themselves have served.

Develop a set of code words with each other and if you're having a particularly bad day – use the word and act accordingly ... don't risk aggravating each other ... it doesn't help in the long run and can do irreparable damage to a relationship. Some people call this 'walking on eggshells' - I disagree ... just look upon it as being thoughtful and considerate of a loved one's problems.

Interviewing Veterans

There are certain things that I would ask you to keep in mind when interviewing Veterans, whatever your role in their life.

Make sure you allow them to sit where they are comfortable. I don't like my back to a door or a window. If I find myself in such a position, most of my awareness is concentrated in those areas because my experiences suggest that I could be vulnerable to an attack from those zones. However, an ex-Navy friend has the opposite reaction, he wanted to be close to a door so that he could exit quickly should the vessel he served on start sinking. We have survived different experiences, so please be flexible and let the Veteran choose his or her safe spot in the room.

Some Veterans swear when they are upset. They won't generally swear at you – unless you do something to warrant the treatment – they're merely venting frustration over a situation that they have been involved in. Let them vent and get it out of their system as they may then calm down sufficiently to allow the interviewer to continue with his or her work. Don't EVER terminate the interview because of this behaviour, unless of course they are actually venting directly at you and you feel that you could be physically harmed by them.

If a person is upset, don't raise your voice to challenge theirs. Stay quiet and let them run out of steam … don't do anything to inflame the situation. Continue the interview when they calm down. Remember that it's your job as the interviewer to build that bridge with the person that you're interviewing … don't collapse it … be flexible and maintain it. Trust in such scenarios is not easily earned.

Remember that if you've facilitated an interview that touches on the Veteran's experience related to his or her service that they may now feel like a primed bomb. Be human and help them to get the lid back on the situation before letting them go home.

Other areas of concern

If you are a Veteran and you're being interviewed about your disability benefits, NEVER go alone, always insist that the interview is recorded and ensure that the person is medically qualified to diagnose you – Eg a General Physician cannot diagnose you with PTSD. Ask the examiner to prove their credentials.

Always try to get appropriate help before going to an interview. You can get help from a Law Centre, Royal British Legion rep or a Welfare Rights Unit. Unfortunately, some examiners are not objective and they do have a hidden agenda – to ensure that you don't receive the benefits that you may be due.

If you transfer from one part of the country to another, make sure your current care providers provide you with up-to-date medical reports for your new care providers.

I guess that's all I have to share on the raising awareness side of things now. Please do keep any eye on my website for changes and updates: www.wolf-photography.com.

Please be aware that most of the Government's efforts with regard to supporting Veterans with PTSD are aimed at survivors of recent conflicts (Ie Iraq and Afghanistan). We still have many unsupported Veterans from World War Two onwards; 15% of the current UK prison population are Veterans and 25% of homeless people in the UK are also Veterans. I would venture that a high proportion of these people live with undiagnosed PTSD.

The Exhibition Layout

The Poems

Those of you that have read my poetry books will be aware of the issues that I write about - the lighter and warmer moments as well as the PTSD (Post Traumatic Stress Disorder) related issues.

However to underline the aims of my project - to raise awareness of PTSD and promote creative arts as a coping mechanism for disability – I wanted to use the more relevant poems to represent the effects of PTSD on my core and to demonstrate how photography helps me to venture out and create images based on my connection with the Earth and some people from other cultures.

If everything goes to plan, there will be a central column of poetry at the venue in Leicester, and the photography will be on the walls around you. So you'll have a chance to walk in my moccasins for a while.

All of the images connected with this project are in this book and follow the poems. I hope that you'll enjoy viewing them.

I'm actually writing this book on Monday 21st October 2013 and the timing's a tad tight! Will the books be live for the opening night on Tuesday 5th November 2013? Fingers crossed!

Province of Dreams

Memories of uniforms and rifles, bricks and bottles.
Mates suffering in silence, on the edge.
VCPs, patrols, stop and searches.
Invincibility of youth cloaking fears of death.
Staring in the darkness, waiting for the round,
While your oppo freezes and goes to the ground.
Memories of racism going unchallenged,
Until your mates spoke up.
Memories of piss-ups and the darkest of humour,
Dealing with the fear as if it's a tumour,
Leaving you cold, functioning like a machine,
Until you wake up with a silent scream.

Tears fall on your pillow.

Memories of the time when your two years were nearly
up,
Feeling the cold steel against your temple.
Memories of things you've done since to fit in,
To come back to life and leave the bad dream.
Making yourself live in the present for your son and your daughter;

Waiting for death.

Forgotten heroes

After the silence,
After the stillness,
After the lonely bugle has sounded.

After march past,
After the memories,
After the door to those feelings close.

They won't remember,
In the halls of power,
Behind their guarded mansion walls.

That without your courage,
They would have nothing,
You who protected their lands.

Whether you're in a cell,
Or cardboard boxes,
Or the prison of an emotional hell.

Hold your head up,
Wherever this day finds you.
We remember your sacrifice.

Am I an old fart?

My arse fits my jeans or trousers
And I don't wear my pants around my knees.
I open doors for ladies or anyone.
I don't call everyone babe or hun.
I don't end every sentence with 'Innit!'
I tell the truth if you ask me a question,
Whether you want it or not.
I don't dribble when I eat or drink, yet!
I can still hold on to a fart with my buns of steel,
If I want to.
I can see wonder and joy in the smallest thing.
I don't expect everyone to like me,
And I won't hold it against you if you don't.
I am not afraid to state a preference.
I'm okay with a label if it helps you,
Just don't try to ram it down my throat.
I don't watch TV,
Preferring to try to live my life than anothers.
I can laugh at silly things,
Just like my kids,
Or splash them at the beach before they soak me!
I can still keep to the beat of the drum,
Or the bass.
I can smile at the happiness of others,
And celebrate their joy and well being.
I am not afraid to cry.
My undies stay inside my pants!
Am I an old fart?

When they come back

Will you stand by them?
The young who fall for you?
The ones who are chased in the halls of dreams,
By memories of things they have seen.

When you see old, haunted eyes in a young face,
Will you wonder why or just pass them by?
When they can't join your society,
For being able to see the truth of it will you cast them further away?

Your world relies on fast food, newest cars and coolest trainers,
Big brand names and the system's retainers.
Theirs on the disciplined bullet and the blind bomb.
Their young emotions locked in a tomb.

Most of them don't like the thought of having to take life.
Didn't like having to witness such strife.
Most of them went out to keep a peace,
Darkness and loneliness is now their disease.

Is it a job you could have done?
But you want the illusion of this 'freedom'.
Your world is grey, nature is white and black.
Will you stand by them when they come back?

Veteran

When you've done your duty by Queen & Country,
When you've risked your all to get the job done,
When you've not taken the shortcuts or dodged the tough jobs,
When you've been abandoned after your service finished,
When you've spent years trying to fit back into a society that doesn't
want you,
When you have to bare your soul to get help,
When your failing memory betrays what your needs are,
When everything is limited by the ticking of a clock,
When there are more casualties than the 'system' wants
to cope with,
When you're scored against each other rather than what
you need,
When your shyness keeps you in the corner,
When the system keeps moving your name to different
boxes,
When your mistrust of society keeps you in the shadows,
When you've had the treatment and the nightmares persist,
When all they'll suggest is to try filling you with pills,
When you go back to your empty home ...

You'll be a Veteran.

Searching

His eyes glisten in the light of the Moon,
As memories intrude upon the peace of the night,
Casting shadows upon the light of his soul.

He raises his muzzle and his sound echoes through the
mountains,
But no other voices join his,
And there is no chorus.
The silence of the mountain swallows his song.

He walks on, searching for his pack.

Your Rules

You made ridiculous rules of engagement.
Your rules put us at risk.
Your rules allowed murderers, gangsters and drug pedlars to go free.
Your rules undermined all our efforts as the combined armed forces
of this nation.
Your rules dishonoured every oath that we took before the flag.
Your agreements feathered your own nests,
And we were the collateral damage,
Expendable souls to be traded in your secret game.
Sooner or later, you will fall foul of your own rules.

Live in the Sun

I live in the shadows of my past,
I try to play in the Sun whenever I can,
But I get burnt at times and retreat to the shadows.

Your presence drew me into the Sun again,
After a long absence.

Your voices caressed my soul in ways I can't yet explain.
Touching the strands of shadow that hold me back,
Making them release their hold on me.
Please be a real presence in my life?
I want to live in the Sun.

The shadows will always be there,
And the scars will need washing from time to time,
But you make me feel that I can do this...
And still live in the Sun.

Acceptable Lies

I won't sneak up on you and tickle you 'til your sides hurt
with laughter.
I won't splash you by jumping high into a puddle we pass on a rainy
day.
I won't make faces at you when I see you frown.
I won't put on a silly voice in the middle of a dance.
These are the only lies I'll ever have told you,
And if you remember that,
The rest will always be the truth.

Circling the Drain

Sitting here in silence, I wait.
The call for help unanswered.
One by one the chains that hold me to this existence snap
And I'm circling the drain;
My feet can't find the earth,
My fingers slide down the slippery slope.
I sit here alone, hope seems to have gone.

What do you do when the system's failing you?
Cause a scene, create a fuss?
These actions are alien to my persona.
I still recognise 'me' in the mirror.
I see the tortured child forged in the fires of rejection,
The teenager that escaped an abusive home.
I see the young man who risked his life to protect others,
Only to be burned for having a sense of honour.

The man that I became through countless baptisms of pain,
Was the man that fought hard for all those that asked it.
Using the energy made from the anger of injustice,
racism and rejection.
I fought hard for you,
To bring some justice to a corrupt society.
But when I have risked my all and sit here depleted,
As my spirit swirls in this whirlpool of pain,
As I see in my mind's eye that I'm being bruised and battered,
The skin scraped from my being,
My wounds raw and exposed,
The words 'help me' feel torn from my throat and die on the wind.

Why won't you help me as I circle the drain?
I paid a price to help you.
You didn't have to ask, I gave freely.
All you seem to see is what I project from the outside.
I'm conditioned to hide my vulnerabilities and fears.
You only see what can be easily ignored or explained,
You don't take the time to find me.
Just another veteran circling the drain.

Bottles and Bricks

The sun is shining, the sky is blue.
The silence is sudden and tangible,
The birds stop singing.
It's as if someone pushed pause on the video.
As if by magic a crowd appears across the road,
Parents stand behind their children.
The first brick sails through the air towards my head,
I casually slip to my left and it misses me.
I focus on the crowd watching for a petrol bomb,
While signalling my oppo to call for back up.
My hand reaches down and I free the pistol from my
holster,
Chambering a round in case I see a legit target.

Parents are throwing bottles and bricks, teaching their kids how,
The kids are smiling as they mimic their parents,
Echoing shouts of 'Feck off home, we don't want yous
here.'
'Catch this you English bastard!'
I smile to myself as I consider my ethnicity.

I continually scan all of them,
A thousand thoughts go through my mind at the same
time,
Am I cleared to open fire?
Not until I see a weapon or a petrol bomb.
If I have to open fire will the round go through my target?
Will it hit an innocent? The brain keeps storming.

I duck inside the shelter to my left and watch and listen,
Bricks, stones and bottles hit the shelter,
Glass splinters around me. I tense for a sprint toward the crowd.

I hear the patrol land rovers screaming towards us,
The crowd runs off behind the fisheries,
I give chase but they've reached safety.
The patrols hit the ground ready to chase the crowd,
Young, determined faces with their emotions locked down.

'Forget it,' I hear my voice say,
'We can't go into the Holiday Homes. Orders.'
I return to my post as the patrol heads off.
I make my weapon safe.
My oppo sticks his head out of the bunker,
'You okay'? I look up and smile the empty smile,
'Fuckin' peachy.'

The birds start singing again.

War is Theft

Theft of innocence
Theft of dignity
Theft of fathers
Theft of mothers
Theft of daughters
Theft of sons
Theft of love
Theft of laughter
Theft of nature
Theft of land
Theft of food
Theft of oil
Theft of gas
Theft of truth
Theft of honour
Theft of life

War is theft

Then and now

Not related by blood,
Not bound by the colour of our skin,
We don't support the same teams,
Or drink the same poison.
Just people that ended up together,
Bound by fate.

I have no brother,
And no sister.
No father,
And no mother,
just this motley crew.

It hurt to leave,
This family of strays,
That were closer than blood.
Our lives in each other's hands,
With one common goal,
To get home again, safe.

I'm back, there is no home.

I have no brother,
And no sister.
No father,
And no mother,
Not even the motley crew.

Killing and fighting

They kill any sense in your head,
They kill your education,
They kill the right to decide,
And They kill the humanity in you.

You kill in the name of Allah,
You kill in the name of God,
You kill for 53 virgins,
And you for a pint of grog.

We kill the future,
We kill communities.
We kill trust,
And we kill innocence.

I try to fight the triggers,
I try to fight the memories,
I try to fight pain within,
and I try to fight their influence.

2 minutes

During the 2 minutes you'll, maybe, remember some of us.
The years of silence our memories still sentence us to,
You'll forget.

The unspoken wound that can't be seen,
Carrying the memories of service,
You won't hear.

Standing tall, we'll walk by you,
Never showing the open wounds,
That cut like knives.

2 minutes later, You'll be back to your life.
2 minutes later, We'll still be trying to make sense of ours.
2 minutes later, another November morning will be forgotten.

The other side of the coin

I dress in my uniform, young and proud,
Razor sharp creases, bulled boots,
Beret badge over the left eye,
Another teenager in the ATC.
51 Squadron was my first 'home'.
I walked to the bus stop
And was stopped by an elderly Asian,
'What are you doing in a white man's uniform?'
Memories of division engendered through my parents came to the
fore:
Years of having white and black friends referred to as 'them';
Not being allowed to mix with Asians of different faith;
Always having to sneak off to be with my friends of other races and
cultures.
I looked at the elderly Asian, my voice was quiet and respectful,
'Sir, what are you doing in a 'white man's' country?'

A year after Northern Ireland

It's a year after Northern Ireland and I stand in a darkened doorway,
In a different place and a different uniform.
The game's vaguely familiar,
But the rules seem very different.
Where there was once unconditional backup - black and white,
Now there's a lot of grey.
I don't even know if we're on the same side.
I feel ostracised, untrusted.
Why do they fear the shade of my skin so much?
Why do they fear my unwillingness to twist the truth for evidence?
Why do they fear my drive to protect the vulnerable ones?
Why do they fear my ability to stick at something 'til I know I can do
it?
They place the hurdles before me and I do my best to over come
them.
The hurdles get higher and the nightmares still haunt me.
The last battle rages through me in my sleeping hours,
This battle haunts my waking hours.
Friendship is a commodity here that's tightly controlled.
I'm regarded as suspicious for upholding my values.
To come to their notice I have to shine twice as much as a 'white'
counterpart.
I feel like ground flesh caught between the cogs of two dangerous
wheels:
The oath and the reality of carrying it out.
I'm bloodied and beaten and unsure of who I can trust,
And every shift becomes a struggle,
Then a fight for existence.
With every policeman I challenge I become more vulnerable,
But there's no one to watch my back.
And the silent threats gather in the darkness to meld with the last
battle,
Torturing me,
Not allowing me any rest,
And peace is something that seems to have become unrecognisable.

Black in Blue

We who serve as black in blue,
We fall between the cracks that appear
between our culture and yours.
Welcomed but not wanted within your ranks,
A political exercise to allay the fears of the persecuted.

We who serve as black in blue,
Learn to see beyond your words and policies.
The stark truth of political expediency,
That leaves us at risk ...
For doing the job you recruited us to do.

We who serve as black in blue,
May get to a certain rung in the ladder,
If we're that lucky ...
But expect that you'll always have snipers waiting,
To pick us off before the next rung.

We who serve as black in blue,
That never hesitated to come to you ...
When you shouted 'Urgent Assistance needed now',
Suffered when you closed ranks against us.
It never was a reciprocal arrangement.

We who served as black in blue,
sworn to serve and protect,
Irrespective of race, gender or sexual persuasion,
Or any other barrier that Society creates,
That suffered for our differences ...
At your hands.

We who served as black in blue,
that refused to be corrupted,
Maintaining the Ideals behind the oath,
That served our communities as well as yours,
Only to be hounded out by hatred inspired by racism.

We who served as black in blue with honour...
Maintain a clear conscience,
Putting your treatment of us down to experience.
You've realised though ...
You can't police the nation without us.

I can see you

I can see you when I close my eyes,
But I don't remember your face.
I could walk past you tomorrow and never know you.
Your scent lines my every breath,
Keeping me alive but lost in my waking hours.
Your eyes hold me close to your soul,
Protecting me,
Keeping alive the promise that you're coming to me,
As quickly as you can.

I picked up a pen

I put the rifle down and picked up a pen,
I'm a poet now and then.
I'm not looking for fame or celebrity status,
Just trying to share how I feel.
Trying to shed some light on a fighter's plight,
And share some of my heart,
And my soul.
Maybe it will help you on your road.

Stormy Mind
(Remembrance Day)

Today I'm dangerous,
Today I'm raw.
My emotions broiling in my mind,
Mixing with memories of service.
Memories of treachery,
Memories of injustice.

Today I'm best left alone,
Today I don't trust myself,
The pain is overwhelming,
Tears won't wash it away.
Flashbacks tumble into each other,
Forming an intrusive video.

Today I need understanding,
Today I need acceptance,
Not to be ridiculed,
Not to be patronised.
I need the peace silence brings,
I need to hold myself in the darkness.

This is my country too

All you see is the shade of my skin,
Not the years of service,
Nor commitment to the oath.
My people settled here,
But here I was born,
And this is my country too.

We seem to be invisible to you,
Us Asian brothers,
But we carried a rifle too,
In defence of this realm,
So put aside your suspicion,
This is our country too.

When I see you next and you look into my soul,
Forget our differences,
Focus on the common goal?
I helped keep you safe at home,
And this is my country too.

Give them 2 minutes

Give me 2 minutes,
And I'll give you a vibe,
The silence will raise your hackles,
It's not a spell,
Or a high from a drug,
Just the energy of the moment shared.

Give me 2 minutes,
And I'll tell you a tale,
Of men and women that risked their all for you,
Mostly forgotten,
Remembered by the lonely bugle,
Ignored by the masses.

Give me 2 minutes,
And I'll open your eyes,
You who value democracy,
But know nothing of its nature,
Nor the lies it conceals,
Leaving you blissfully ignorant.

Give them 2 minutes,
They sacrificed their all for you,
Not for political gain,
Not for favours,
Nor a medal,
They did what they believed was right.

Your blood is red

Black, white, brown and yellow,
Your blood is red.
Male, female, post op, transgender,
Your blood is red.
Gay, lesbian, bisexual, straight,
Your blood is red.
Muslim, Christian, Hindu or Jew,
Your blood is red.
Socialist, conservative or ineffective,
Your blood is red.
Soldier, sailor, tinker, tailor,
Your blood is red.
Able, disabled, athletic, couch potato,
Your blood is red.

Should our variety not enrich our commonality?

Human culling

There is a culling system for humans.
It's called war.
Why not learn to live responsibly instead?

The Images

The Left Side

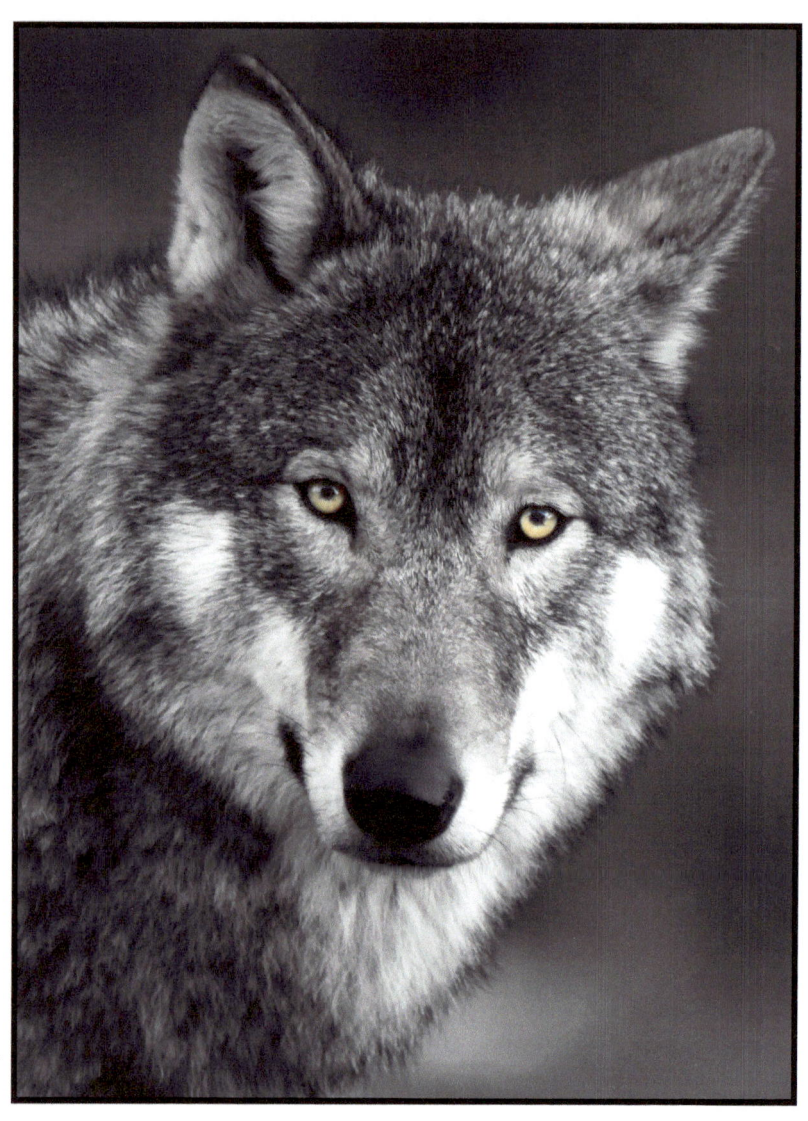

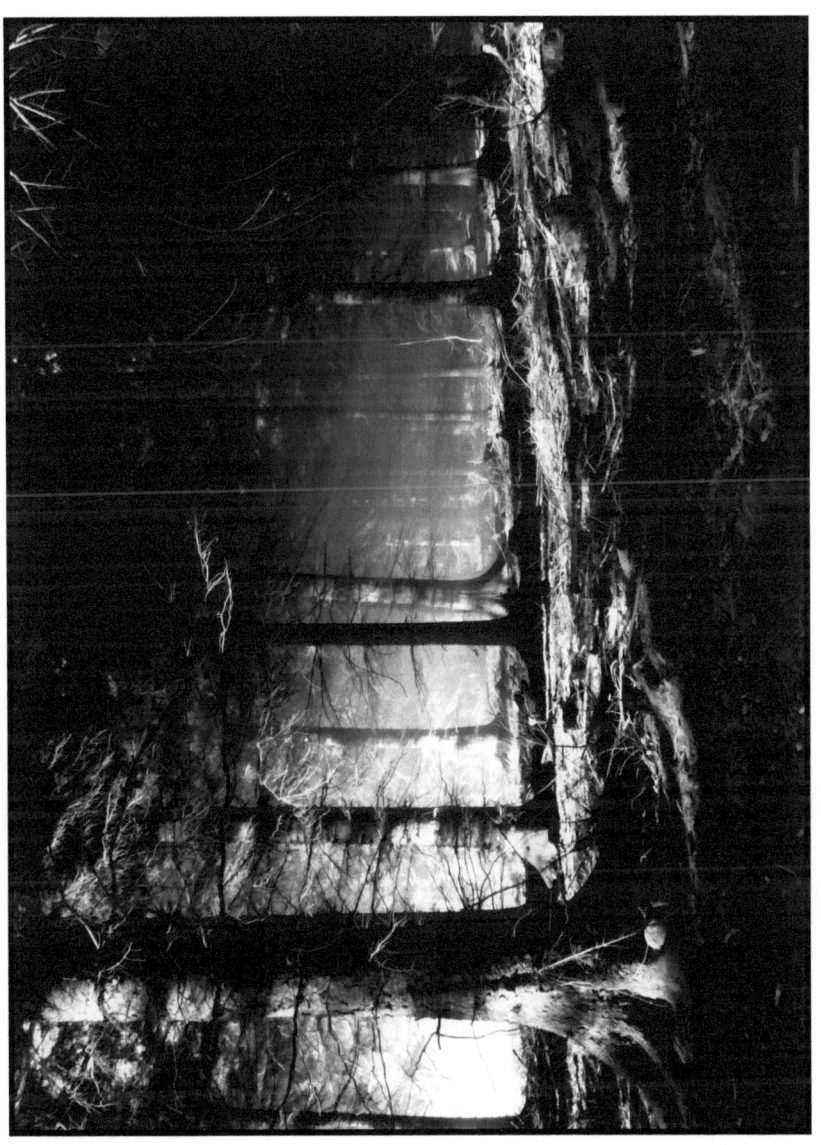

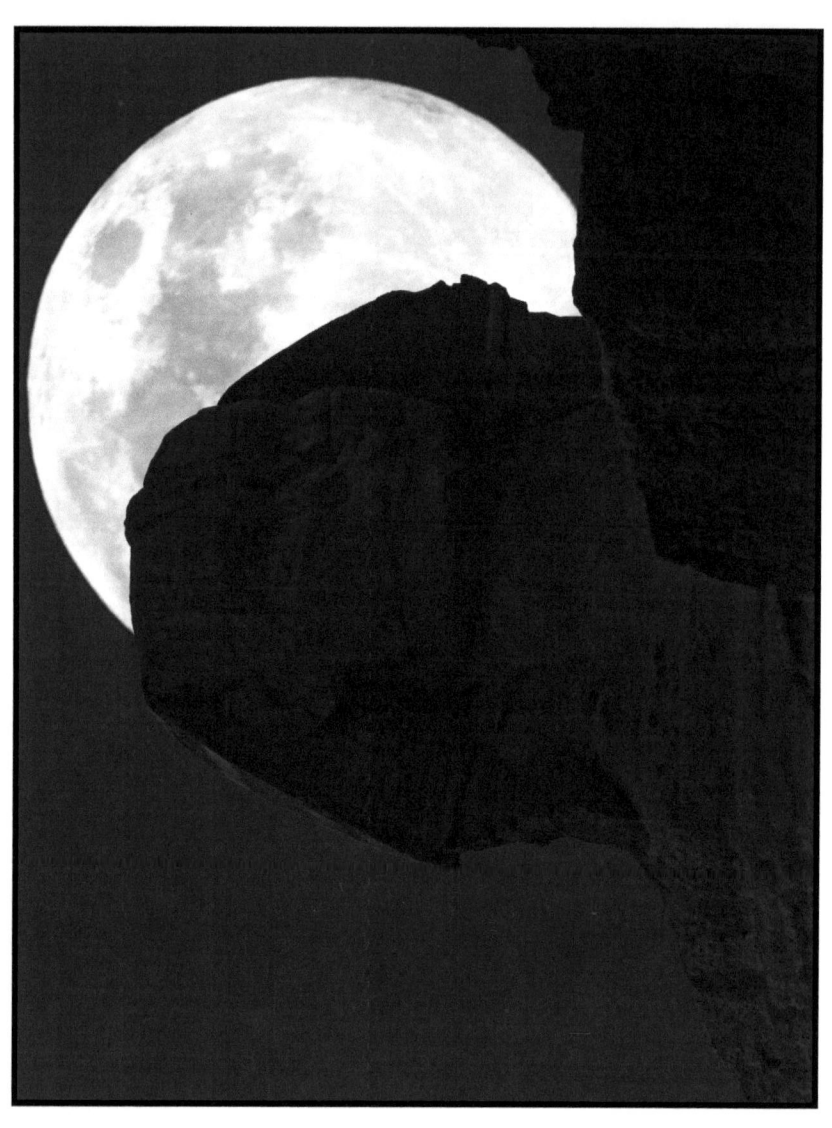

The Front

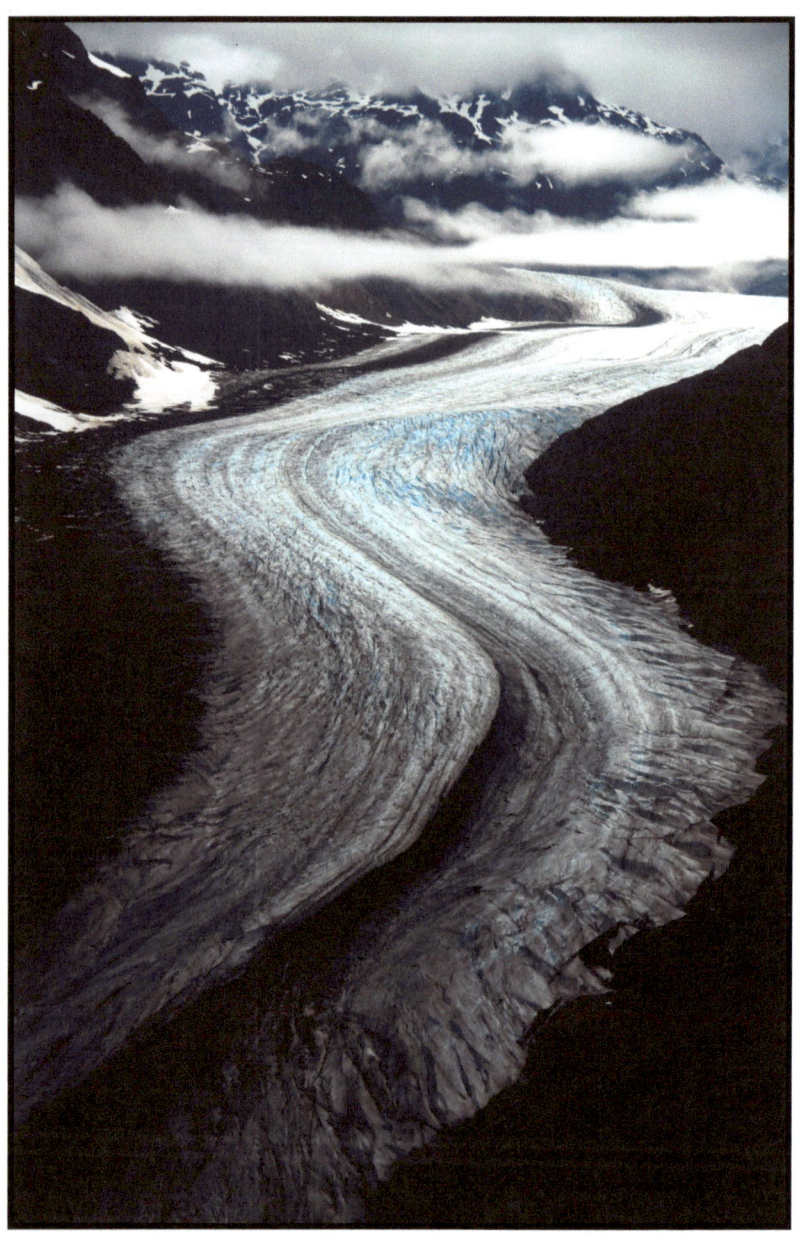

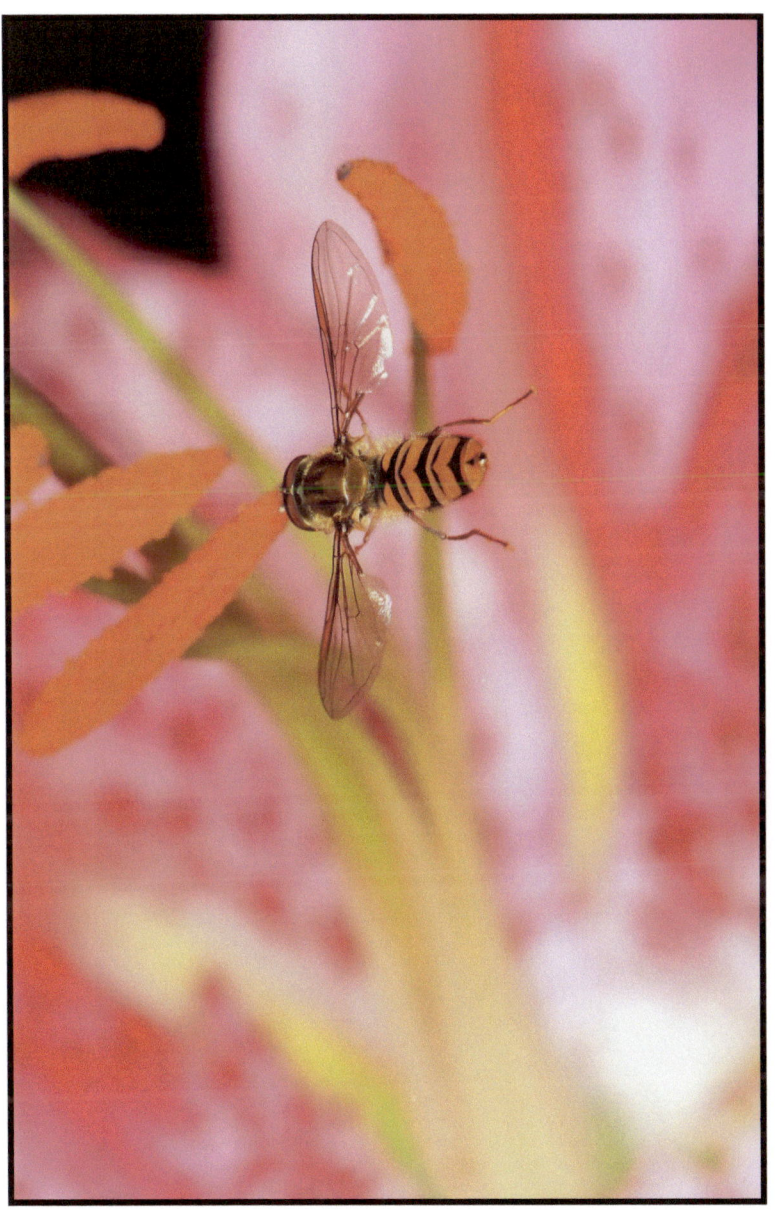

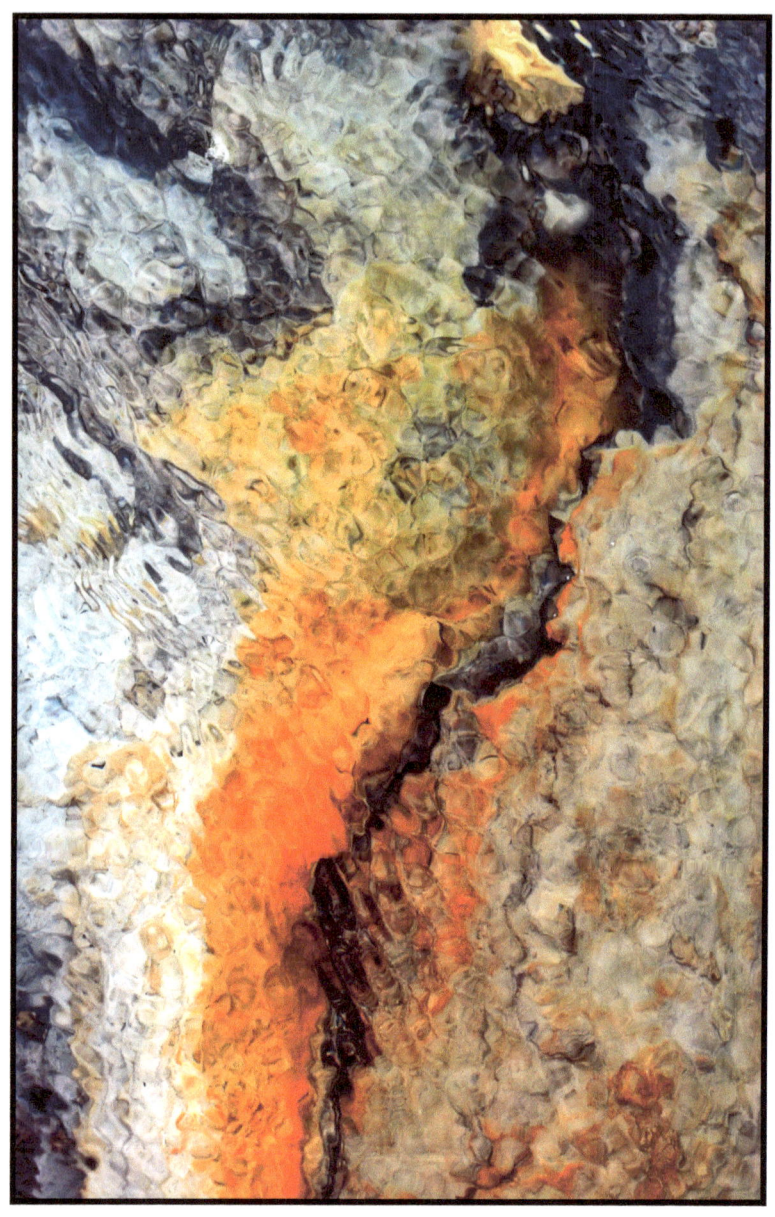

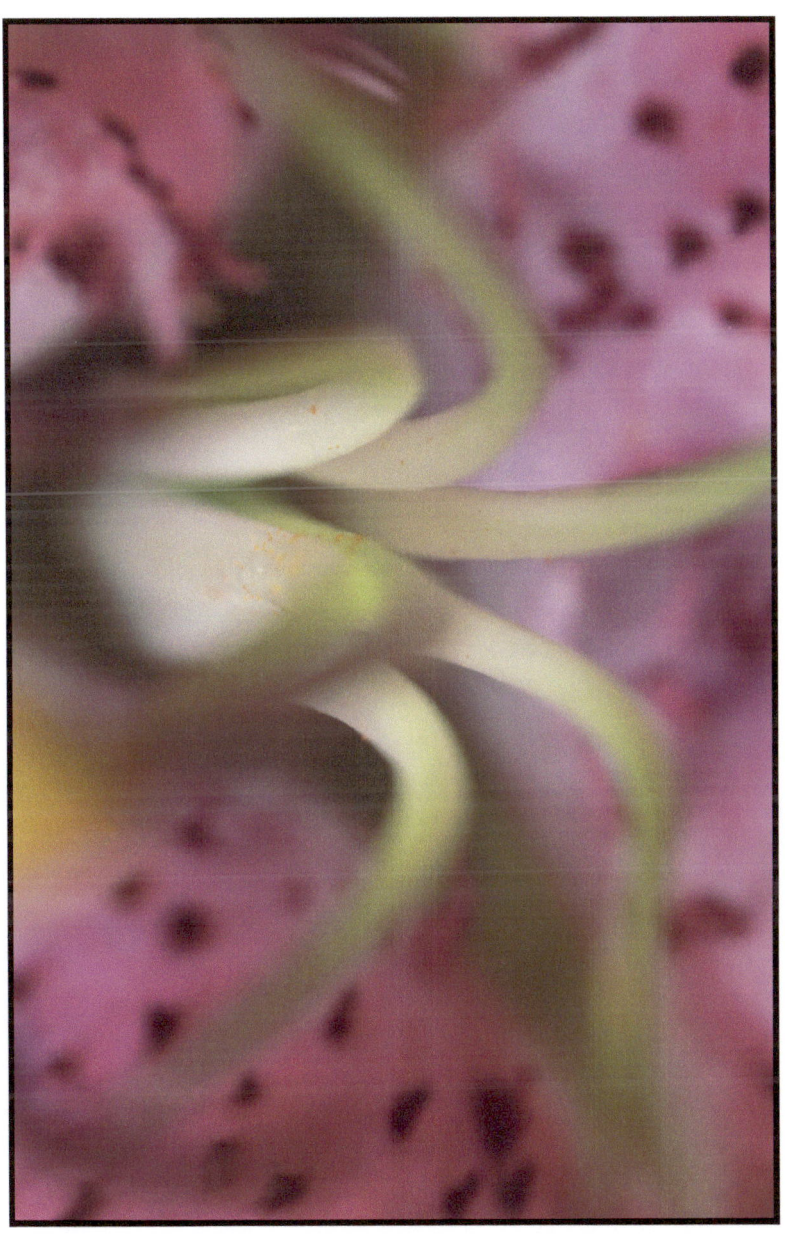

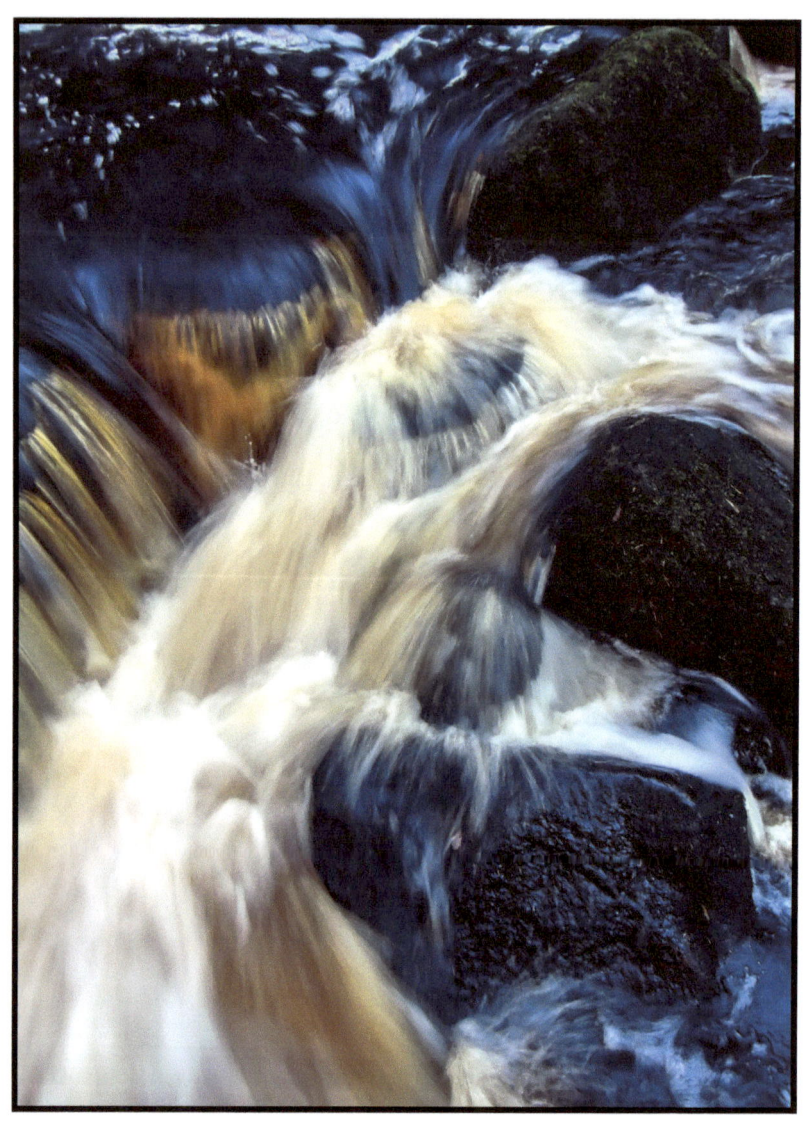

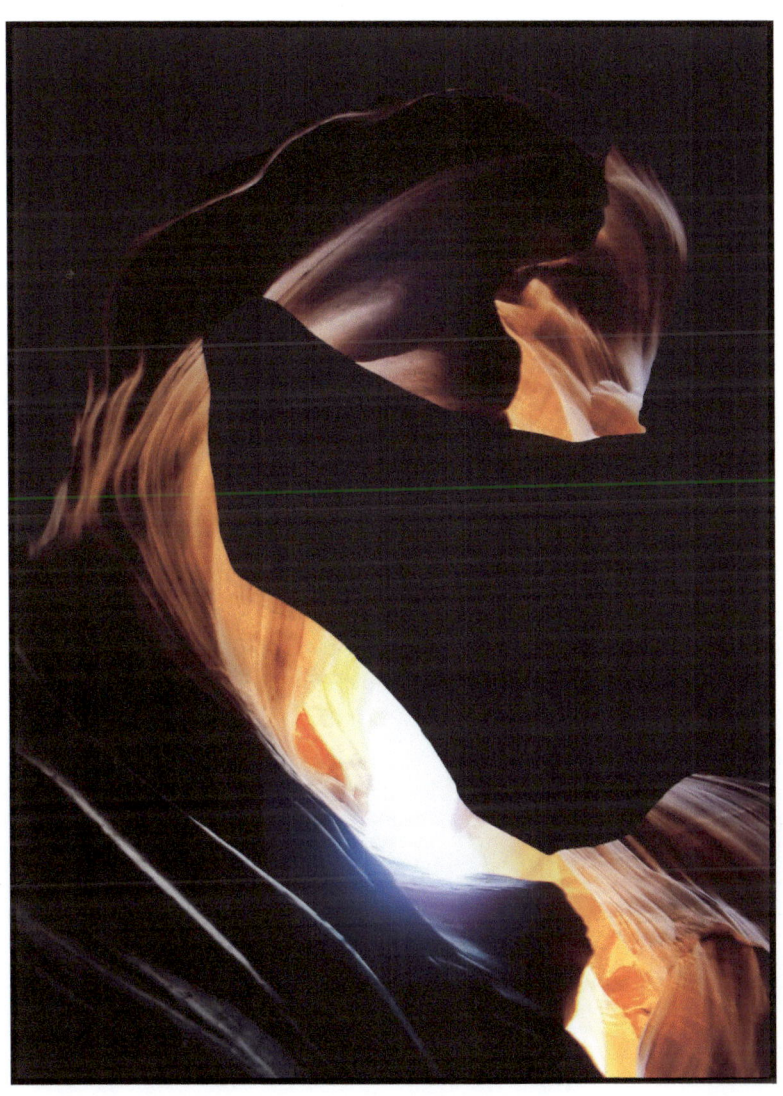

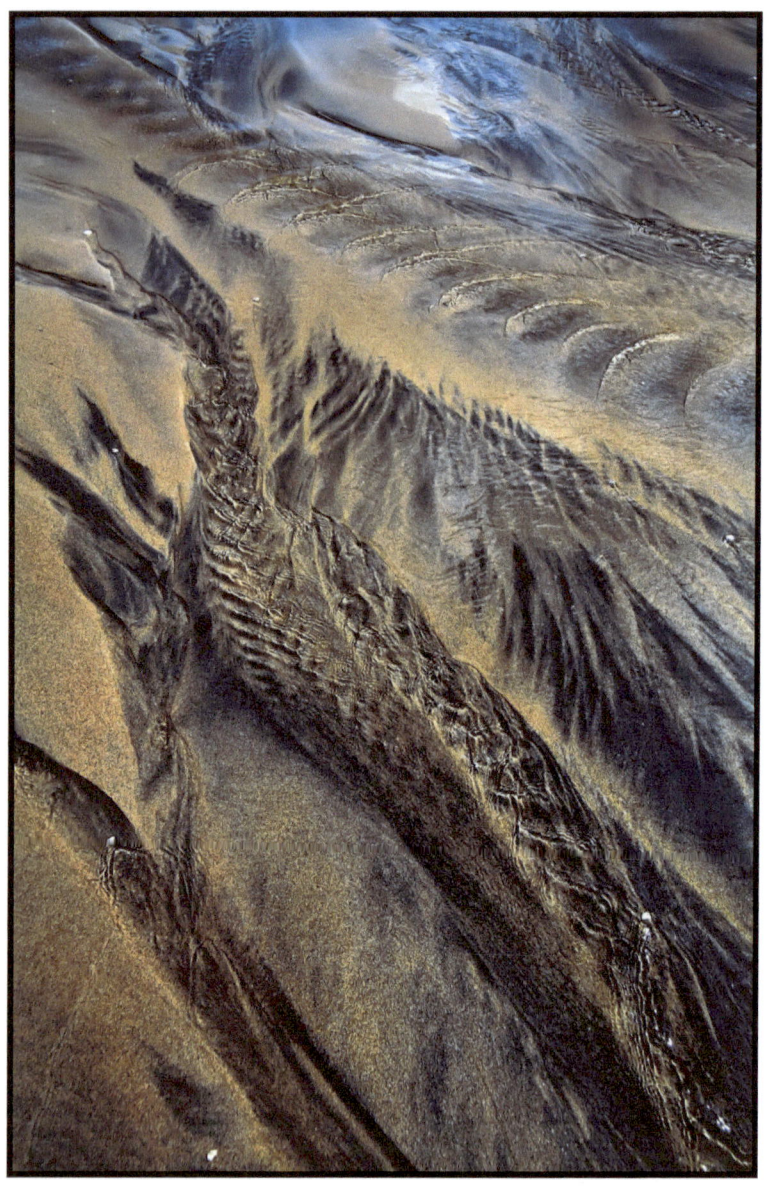

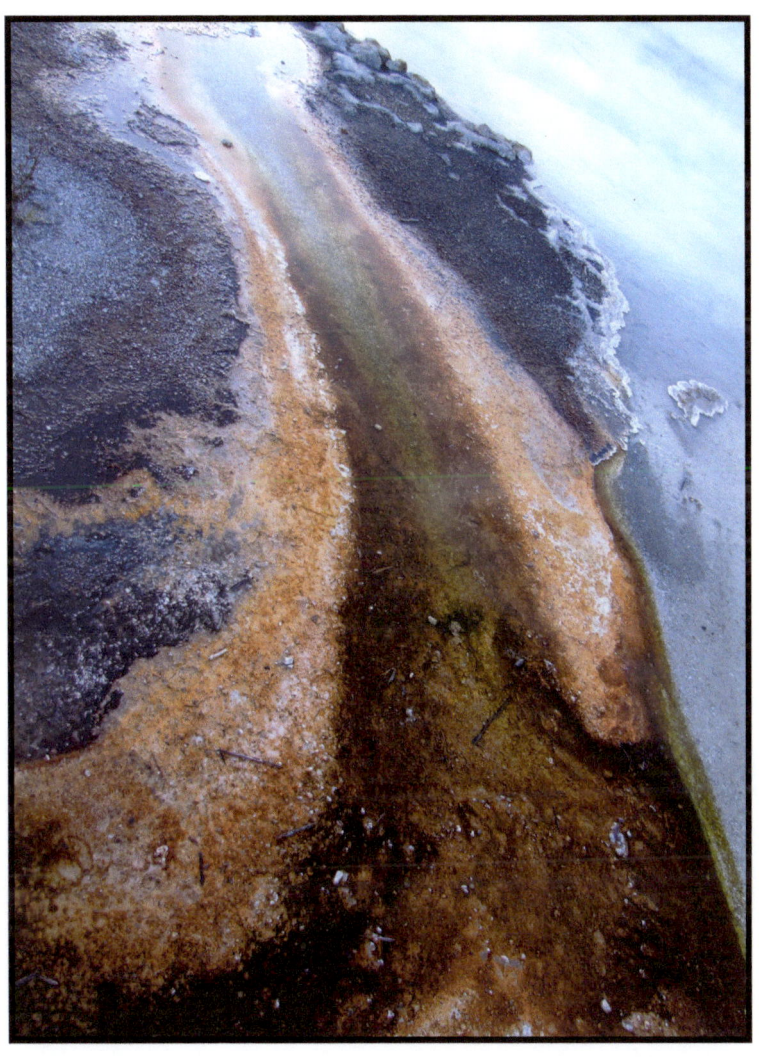

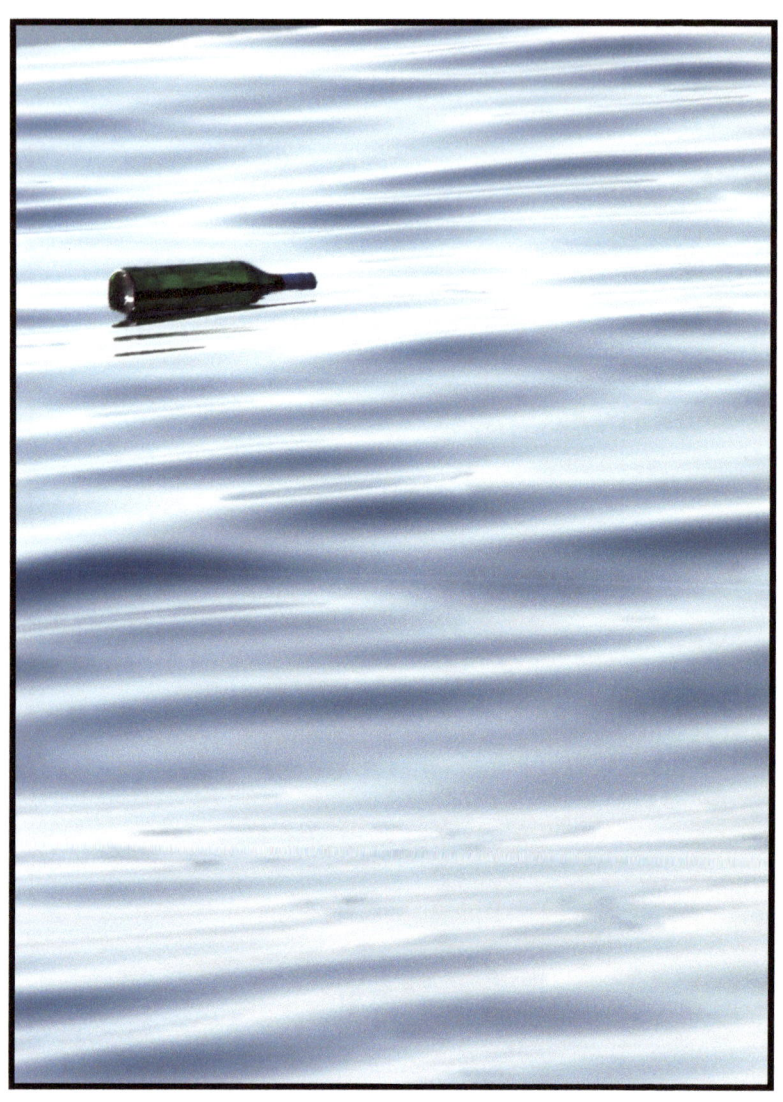

The Right Side

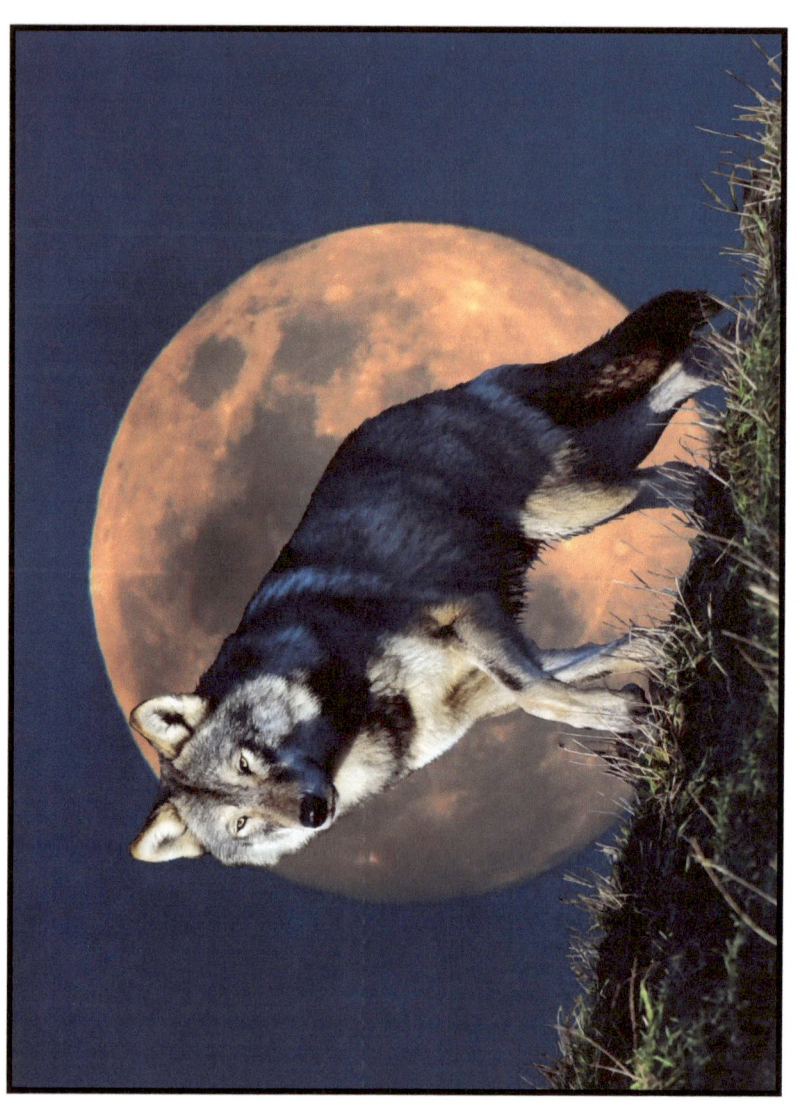

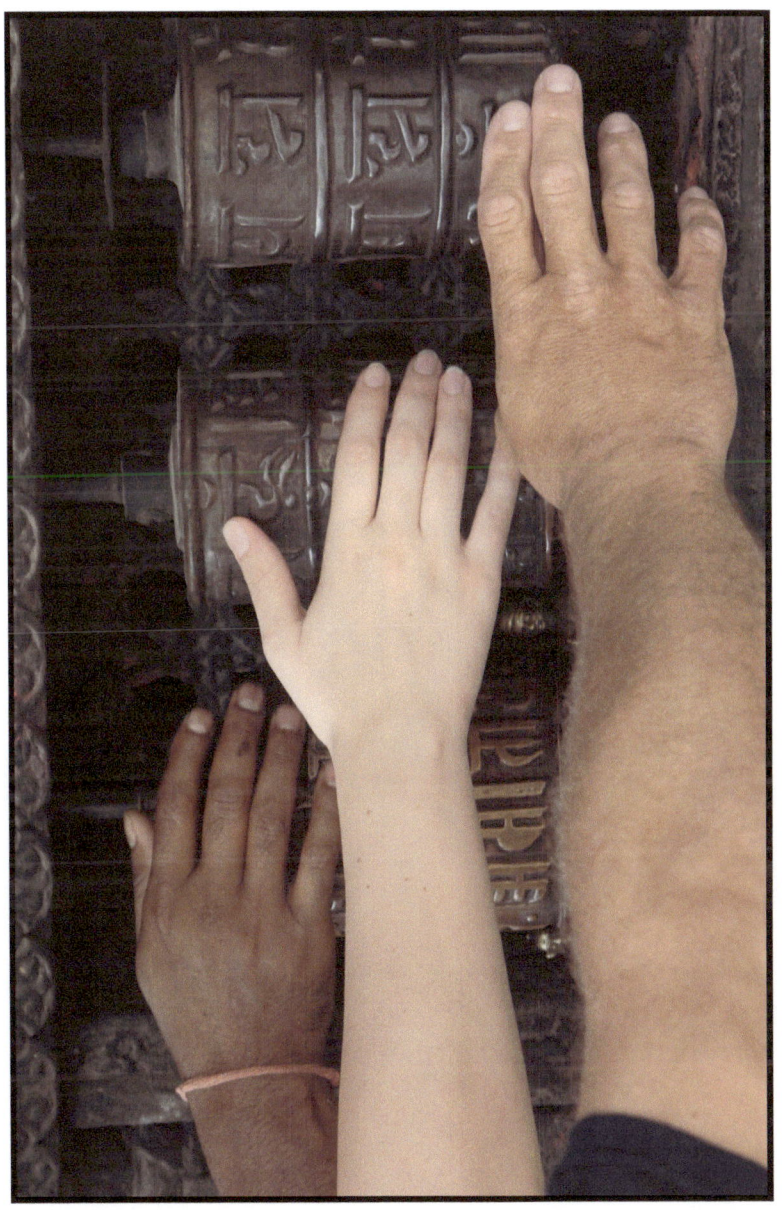

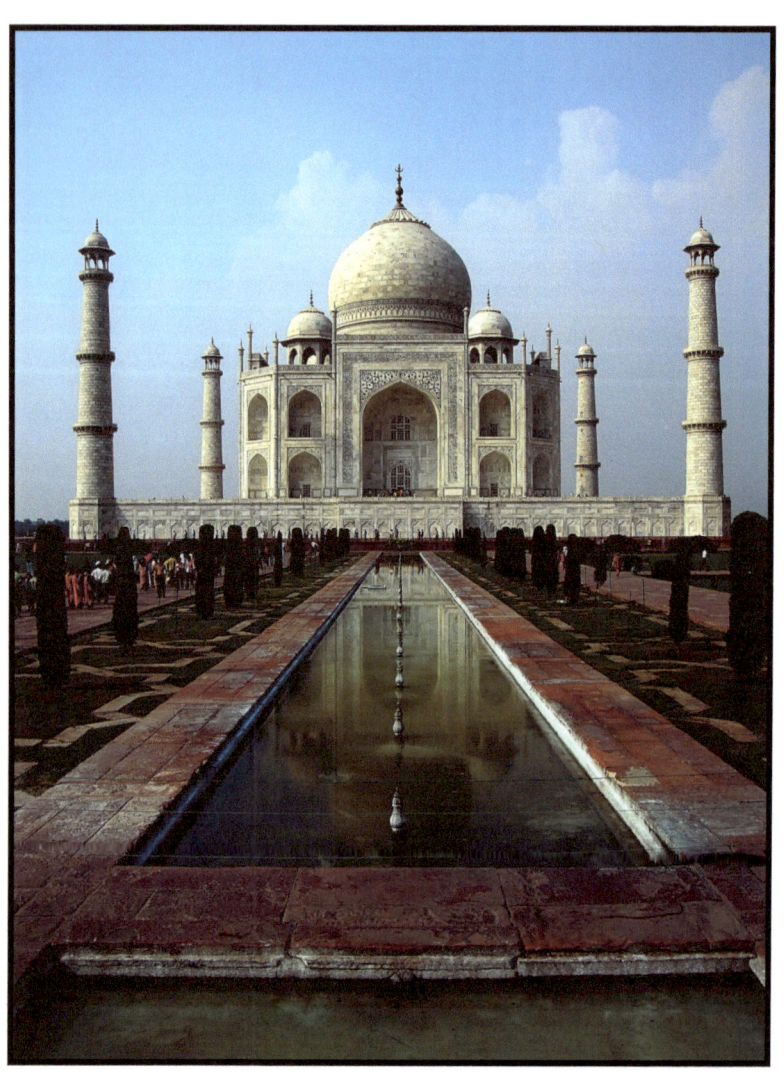

The Back

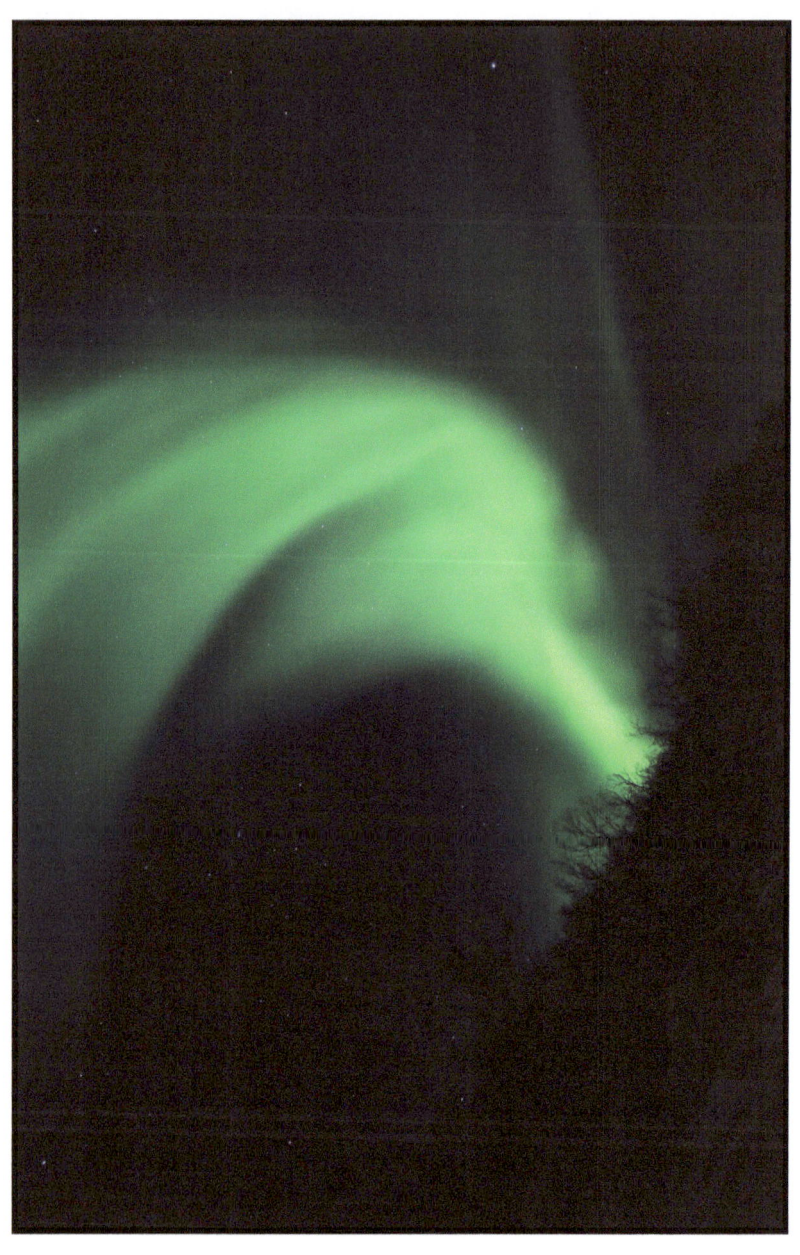

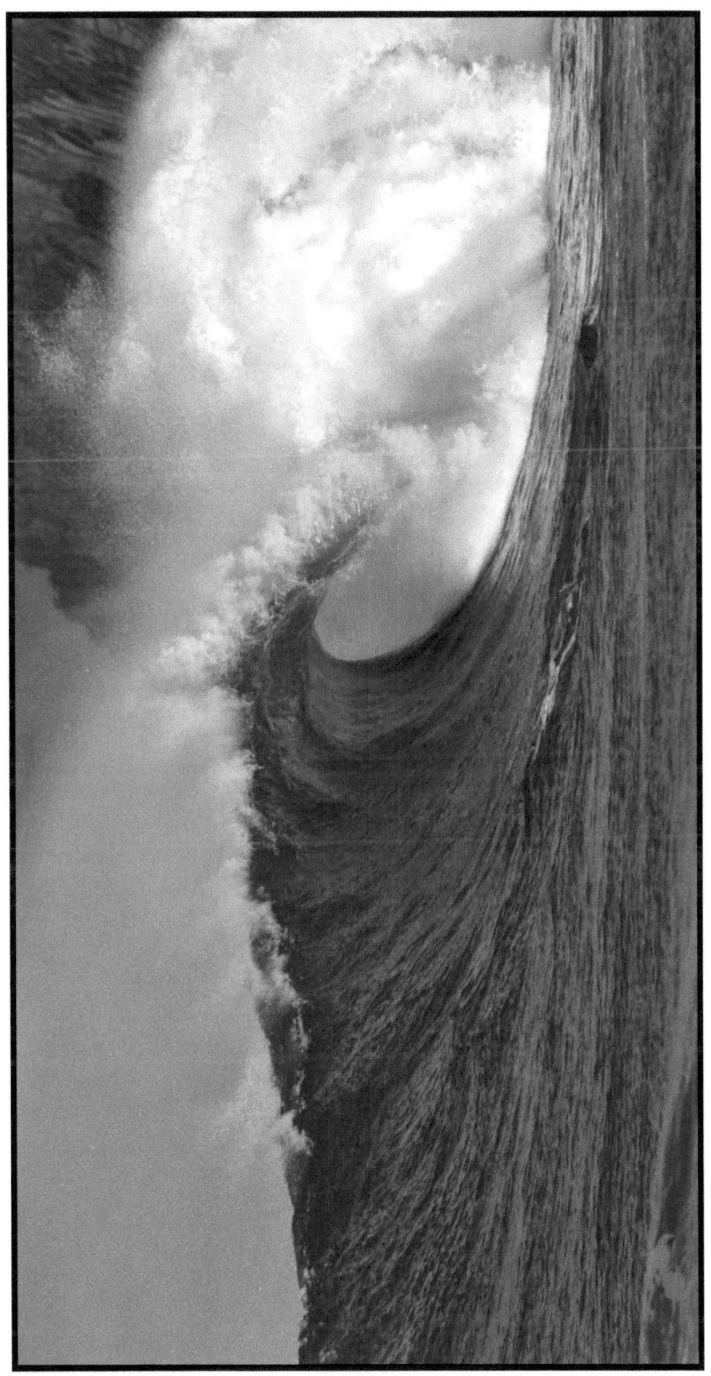

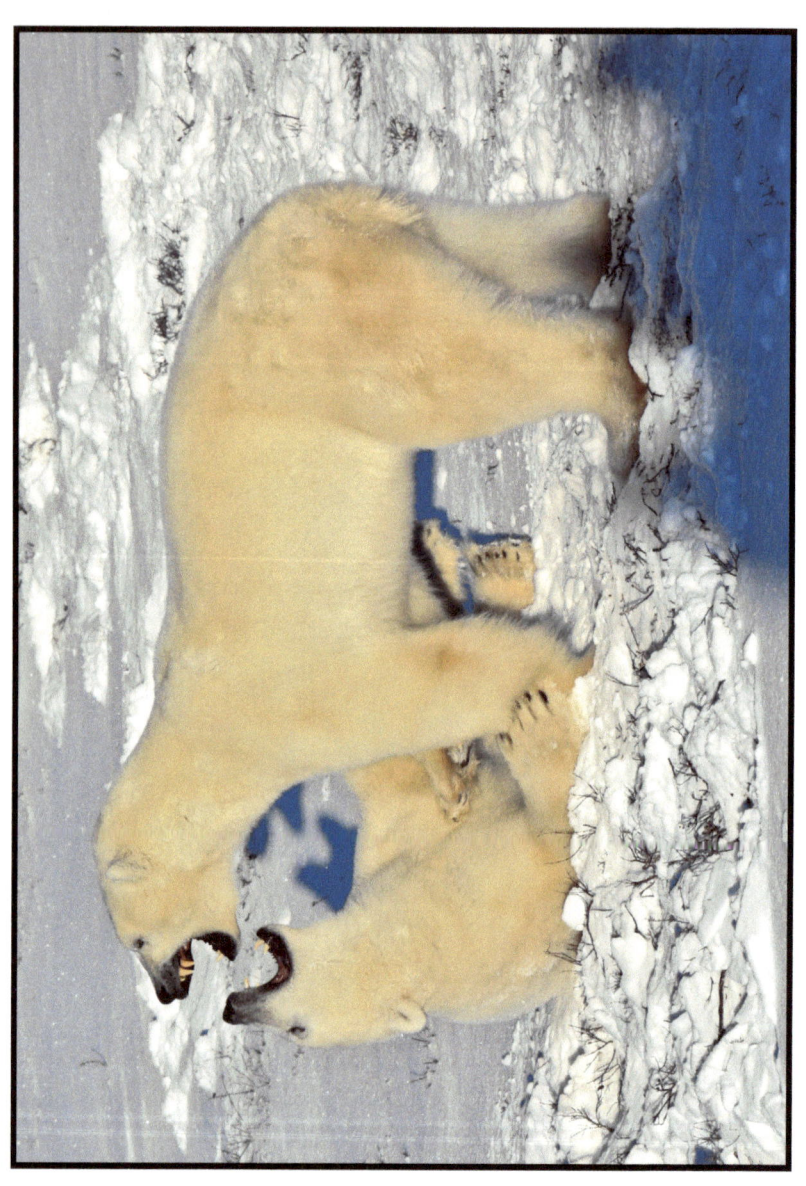

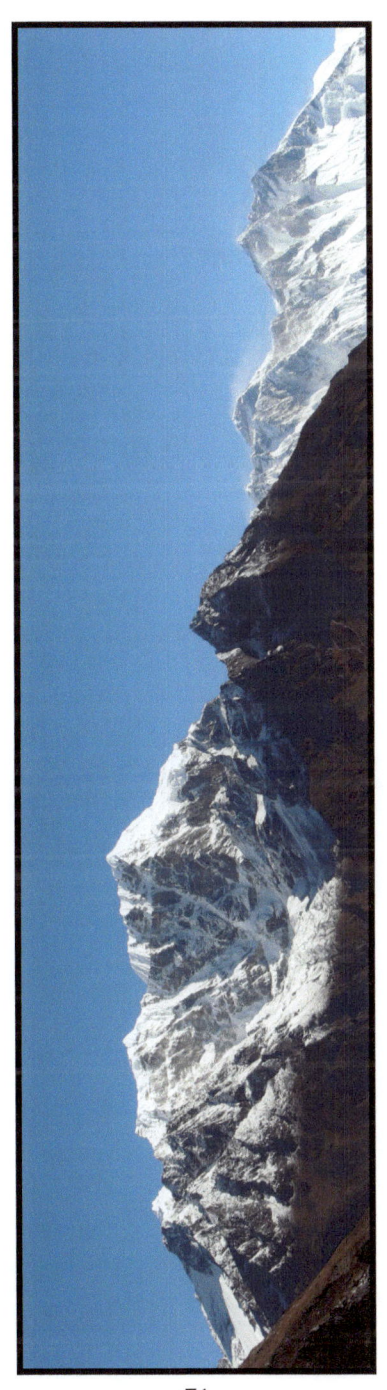

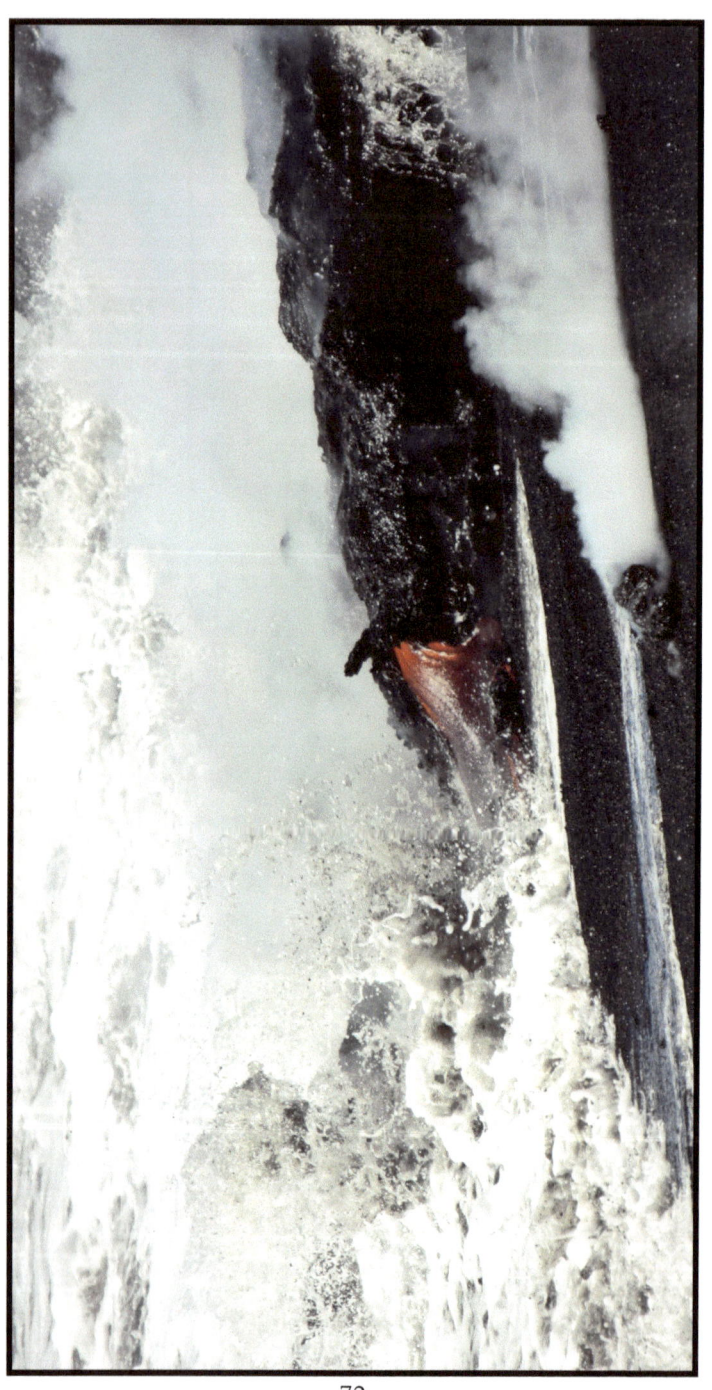

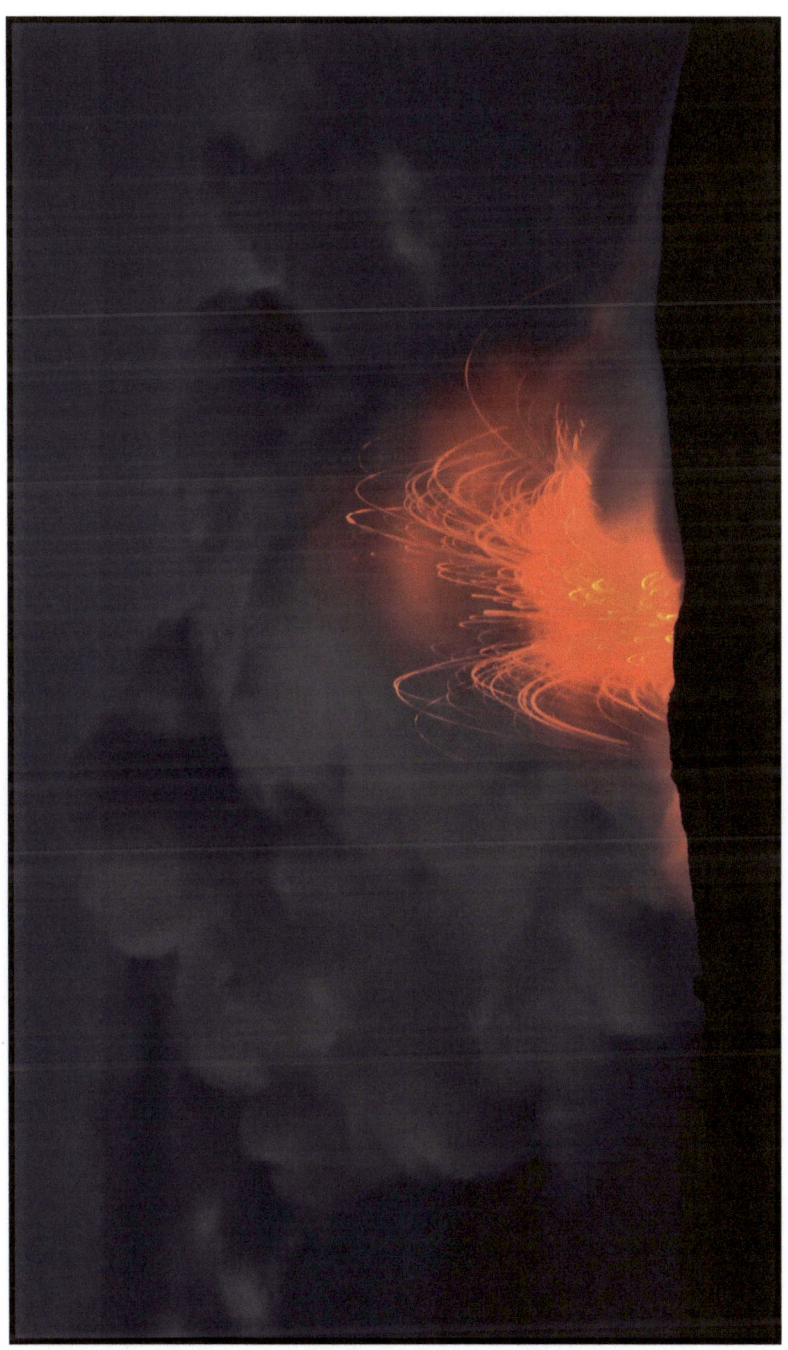

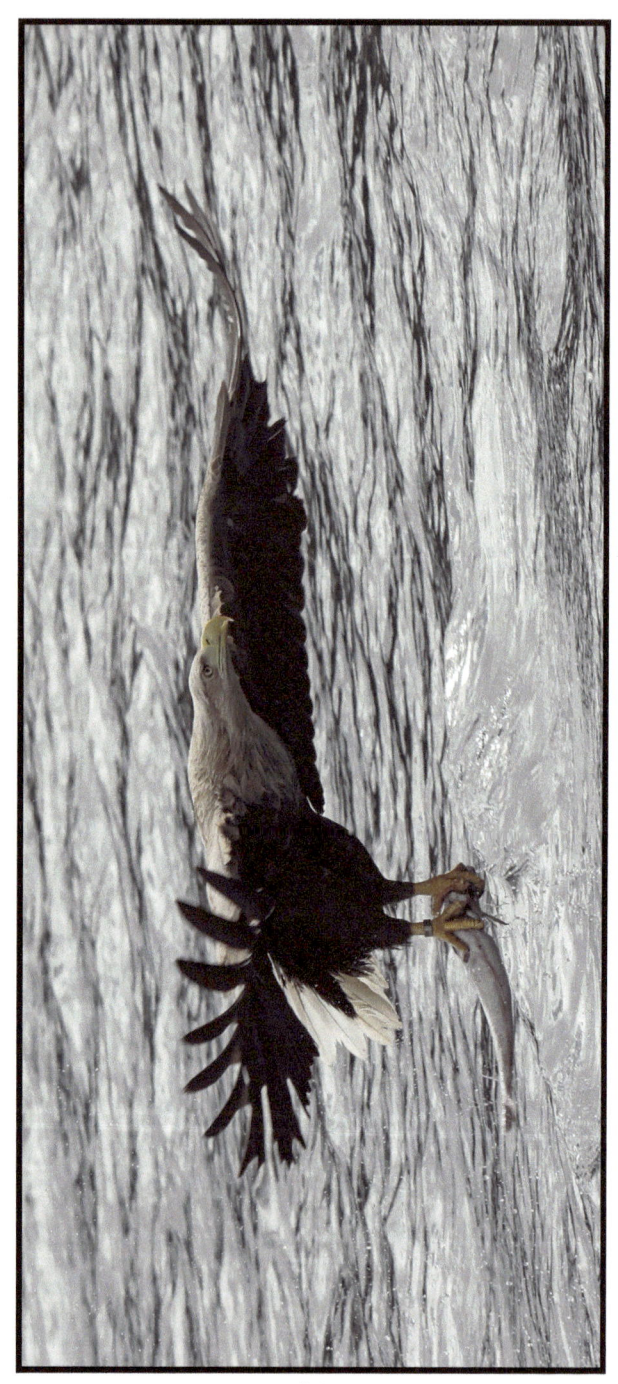

Table of images

Ending thoughts

I hope that you managed to view the exhibition and that you enjoyed it.

I also hope that you've found some of the advice in this book useful.

Please remember that this is a 'rolling exhibition'. I need it to go from place to place so that it can do what it was set up to do – 'raise awareness of PTSD in Veterans'.

If you know of a venue in your town or city that would like to show this exhibition for a month, please get in touch via the website: www.wolf-photography.com.

Thank you for your support!

Mitakuye Oyasin
(translates to: All My Relations – A Lakota Prayer recognising one's relationship with all living things).

Villayat 'SnowMoon Wolf' Sunkmanitu 21 October 2013.

Also by the author

Words of a Wolf
Poetry of a Veteran

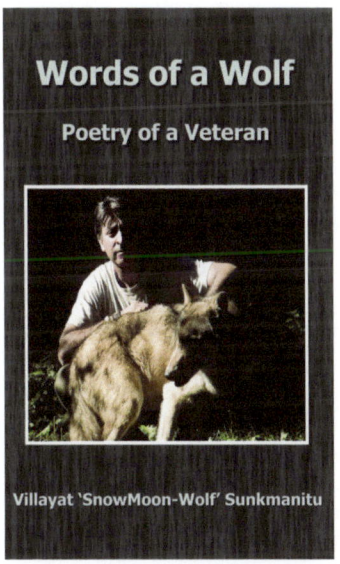

Paperback ISBN: 9780956488503
Kindle ASIN: B0073YE7OQ

The Way of the Wolf
Poetry of a Veteran

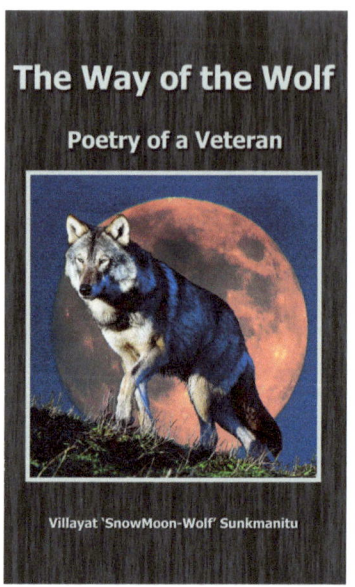

Paperback ISBN: 9780956488527
Kindle ASIN: B0084MQIRU

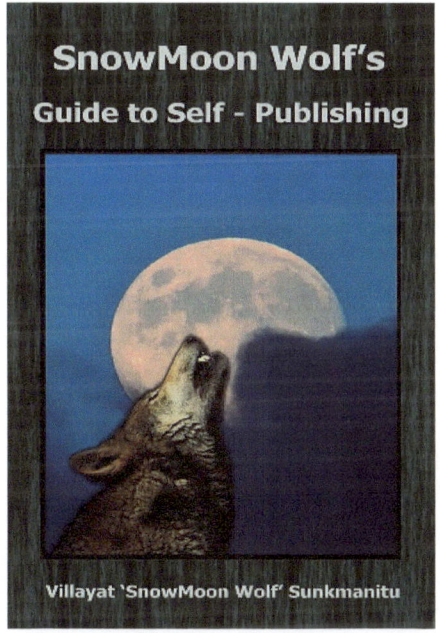

Amazon Kindle ASIN: B008AX14CW

Soul of a Wolf – Poetry of a Veteran

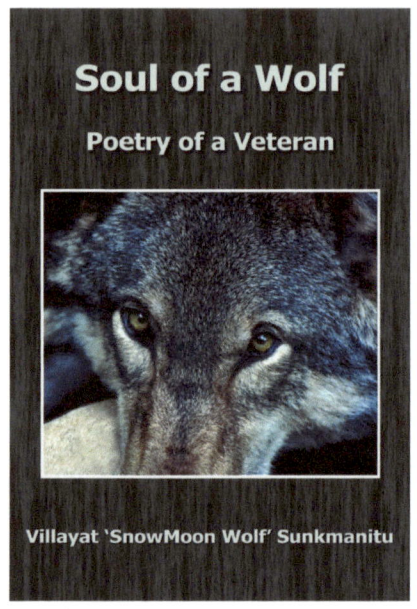

Paperback ISBN: 9780956488596
Amazon Kindle ASIN: B00D0EMUV0

Organisations that can help Veterans

Australia
Department of Veterans' Affairs
(http://www.dva.gov.au/Pages/home.aspx)

Canada
Veterans Affairs Canada (http://www.veterans.gc.ca/eng/)
The Royal Canadian Legion (http://legion.ca/)

UK
Combat Stress (http://www.combatstress.org.uk)
Veterans UK (http://www.veterans-uk.info)
The Royal British Legion (http://www.britishlegion.org.uk/)
SSAFA (http://www.ssafa.org.uk/)
RAF Benevolent Fund (http://www.rafbf.org/)
Army Benevolent Fund
(http://www.soldierscharity.org/)
Royal Naval Benevolent Trust (http://www.rnbt.org.uk/)
The Gurkha Welfare Trust (http://www.gwt.org.uk/)
NHS mental health support for UK Veterans
(http://www.nhs.uk/Livewell/Militarymedicine/Pages/Veteransment
alhealth.aspx)

USA
Department of Veterans Affairs (http://www.va.gov/)

As a UK Veteran it's worth bearing in mind that the countries above
may well be able to help you, if only briefly, by allowing you to talk
should you have a bad episode whilst travelling.

Please support this project

You can help a lot by clicking 'Like' on the project's main Facebook page, Wolf.Photographer, as well as liking and sharing stories and images to your Facebook page.

If you're a Twitter user, please follow 'wolf_photo' and retweet our information and articles.

Please tell your friends and family about the main website as well. Full details are below.

Thank you!

Facebook:

https://www.facebook.com/Wolf.Photographer

Twitter:

https://twitter.com/wolf_photo

Main website:

http://www.wolf-photography.com

Notes